Monthly Oil Business Tracker

Year: _____

Current Rank: _____

Goal Rank: _____

by Jennifer Wallner

January

CALENDAR

Sunday	Monday	Tuesday	Wednesday	Thursday	Friday	Saturday

MONTH AT A GLANCE

POM

10% off

200PV Special

Enrollment Special

LRP Order

To Do List

Booked Classes & One-On-Ones

Personal Goal	Checks
Business Goal	Fast Start #1 $_____
	Fast Start #2 $_____
Mileage	Fast Start #3 $_____
	Fast Start #4 $_____
	Unilevel $_____
Leadership Call	**Mentor Call(s)**
Diamond Call	
New Enrollments	**Rank Advancements**

NOTES

February

CALENDAR

Sunday	Monday	Tuesday	Wednesday	Thursday	Friday	Saturday

MONTH AT A GLANCE

POM

10% off

200PV Special

Enrollment Special

LRP Order

To Do List

Booked Classes & One-On-Ones

Personal Goal	Checks
Business Goal	Fast Start #1 $_____
	Fast Start #2 $_____
Mileage	Fast Start #3 $_____
	Fast Start #4 $_____
	Unilevel $_____
Leadership Call	**Mentor Call(s)**
Diamond Call	
New Enrollments	**Rank Advancements**

NOTES

March

CALENDAR

Sunday	Monday	Tuesday	Wednesday	Thursday	Friday	Saturday

MONTH AT A GLANCE

POM	LRP Order
10% off	
200PV Special	
Enrollment Special	

To Do List	Booked Classes & One-On-Ones

Personal Goal	Checks
Business Goal	Fast Start #1 $_____
	Fast Start #2 $_____
Mileage	Fast Start #3 $_____
	Fast Start #4 $_____
	Unilevel $_____
Leadership Call	**Mentor Call(s)**
Diamond Call	
New Enrollments	**Rank Advancements**

NOTES

April

CALENDAR

Sunday	Monday	Tuesday	Wednesday	Thursday	Friday	Saturday

MONTH AT A GLANCE

POM	LRP Order
10% off	
200PV Special	
Enrollment Special	

To Do List	Booked Classes & One-On-Ones

Personal Goal	Checks
Business Goal	Fast Start #1 $_____
	Fast Start #2 $_____
Mileage	Fast Start #3 $_____
	Fast Start #4 $_____
	Unilevel $_____
Leadership Call	**Mentor Call(s)**
Diamond Call	
New Enrollments	**Rank Advancements**

NOTES

May

CALENDAR

Sunday	Monday	Tuesday	Wednesday	Thursday	Friday	Saturday

MONTH AT A GLANCE

POM

10% off

200PV Special

Enrollment Special

LRP Order

To Do List

Booked Classes & One-On-Ones

Personal Goal

Business Goal

Mileage

Leadership Call

Diamond Call

New Enrollments

Checks

Fast Start #1 $_____

Fast Start #2 $_____

Fast Start #3 $_____

Fast Start #4 $_____

Unilevel $_____

Mentor Call(s)

Rank Advancements

NOTES

June

CALENDAR

Sunday	Monday	Tuesday	Wednesday	Thursday	Friday	Saturday

MONTH AT A GLANCE

POM

10% off

200PV Special

Enrollment Special

LRP Order

To Do List

Booked Classes & One-On-Ones

Personal Goal

Business Goal

Mileage

Leadership Call

Diamond Call

New Enrollments

Checks

Fast Start #1 $_____

Fast Start #2 $_____

Fast Start #3 $_____

Fast Start #4 $_____

Unilevel $_____

Mentor Call(s)

Rank Advancements

NOTES

July

CALENDAR

Sunday	Monday	Tuesday	Wednesday	Thursday	Friday	Saturday

MONTH AT A GLANCE

POM

10% off

200PV Special

Enrollment Special

LRP Order

To Do List

Booked Classes & One-On-Ones

Personal Goal	Checks
Business Goal	Fast Start #1 $_____
	Fast Start #2 $_____
Mileage	Fast Start #3 $_____
	Fast Start #4 $_____
	Unilevel $_____
Leadership Call	**Mentor Call(s)**
Diamond Call	
New Enrollments	**Rank Advancements**

NOTES

August

CALENDAR

Sunday	Monday	Tuesday	Wednesday	Thursday	Friday	Saturday

MONTH AT A GLANCE

POM

10% off

200PV Special

Enrollment Special

LRP Order

To Do List

Booked Classes & One-On-Ones

Personal Goal	Checks
Business Goal	Fast Start #1 $_____
	Fast Start #2 $_____
Mileage	Fast Start #3 $_____
	Fast Start #4 $_____
	Unilevel $_____
Leadership Call	**Mentor Call(s)**
Diamond Call	
New Enrollments	**Rank Advancements**

NOTES

September

CALENDAR

Sunday	Monday	Tuesday	Wednesday	Thursday	Friday	Saturday

MONTH AT A GLANCE

POM

10% off

200PV Special

Enrollment Special

LRP Order

To Do List

Booked Classes & One-On-Ones

Personal Goal

Business Goal

Mileage

Leadership Call

Diamond Call

New Enrollments

Checks

Fast Start #1 $_____

Fast Start #2 $_____

Fast Start #3 $_____

Fast Start #4 $_____

Unilevel $_____

Mentor Call(s)

Rank Advancements

NOTES

October

CALENDAR

Sunday	Monday	Tuesday	Wednesday	Thursday	Friday	Saturday

MONTH AT A GLANCE

POM

10% off

200PV Special

Enrollment Special

LRP Order

To Do List

Booked Classes & One-On-Ones

Personal Goal	Checks
Business Goal	Fast Start #1 $_____
	Fast Start #2 $_____
Mileage	Fast Start #3 $_____
	Fast Start #4 $_____
	Unilevel $_____
Leadership Call	**Mentor Call(s)**
Diamond Call	
New Enrollments	**Rank Advancements**

NOTES

November

CALENDAR

Sunday	Monday	Tuesday	Wednesday	Thursday	Friday	Saturday

MONTH AT A GLANCE

POM

10% off

200PV Special

Enrollment Special

LRP Order

To Do List

Booked Classes & One-On-Ones

Personal Goal

Business Goal

Mileage

Leadership Call

Diamond Call

New Enrollments

Checks

Fast Start #1 $_____

Fast Start #2 $_____

Fast Start #3 $_____

Fast Start #4 $_____

Unilevel $_____

Mentor Call(s)

Rank Advancements

NOTES

December

CALENDAR

Sunday	Monday	Tuesday	Wednesday	Thursday	Friday	Saturday

MONTH AT A GLANCE

POM

10% off

200PV Special

Enrollment Special

LRP Order

To Do List

Booked Classes & One-On-Ones

Personal Goal	Checks
Business Goal	Fast Start #1 $_____
	Fast Start #2 $_____
Mileage	Fast Start #3 $_____
	Fast Start #4 $_____
	Unilevel $_____
Leadership Call	**Mentor Call(s)**
Diamond Call	
New Enrollments	**Rank Advancements**

NOTES

END OF THE YEAR REFLECTION

www.ingramcontent.com/pod-product-compliance
Lightning Source LLC
Chambersburg PA
CBHW080819170526
45158CB00009B/2469